WE THE JURY

ALSO BY WAYNE MILLER

POETRY COLLECTIONS
Post–
The City, Our City
The Book of Props
Only the Senses Sleep

CO-TRANSLATED BOOKS
Zodiac, by Moikom Zeqo
I Don't Believe in Ghosts, by Moikom Zeqo

CO-EDITED BOOKS
Literary Publishing in the Twenty-First Century
Tamura Ryuichi: On the Life & Work of a 20th Century Master
New European Poets

WE THE JURY

POEMS

WAYNE MILLER

MILKWEED EDITIONS

Published 2021 by Milkweed Editions
Printed in Canada
Cover design by Mary Austin Speaker
Cover art by Danny Singer
21 22 23 24 25   5 4 3 2 1
First Edition

Milkweed Editions, an independent nonprofit publisher, gratefully acknowledges
sustaining support from our Board of Directors; the Alan B. Slifka Foundation
and its president, Riva Ariella Ritvo-Slifka; the Amazon Literary Partnership; the
Ballard Spahr Foundation; *Copper Nickel*; the McKnight Foundation; the National
Endowment for the Arts; the National Poetry Series; the Target Foundation; and
other generous contributions from foundations, corporations, and individuals. Also,
this activity is made possible by the voters of Minnesota through a Minnesota State
Arts Board Operating Support grant, thanks to a legislative appropriation from the
arts and cultural heritage fund. For a full listing of Milkweed Editions supporters,
please visit milkweed.org.

Library of Congress Cataloging-in-Publication Data

Names: Miller, Wayne, 1976-, author.
Title: We the jury : poems / Wayne Miller.
Description: First Edition. | Minneapolis, Minnesota : Milkweed Editions,
    [2021] | Summary: "Wayne Miller's fourth collection of poems engages
    with questions of morality without clear answers"-- Provided by
    publisher.
Identifiers: LCCN 2020028691 (print) | LCCN 2020028692 (ebook) | ISBN
    9781571315311 (paperback) | ISBN 9781571317193 (ebook)
Subjects: LCGFT: Poetry.
Classification: LCC PS3613.I56245 W4 2021 (print) | LCC PS3613.I56245
    (ebook) | DDC 811/.6--dc23
LC record available at https://lccn.loc.gov/2020028691
LC ebook record available at https://lccn.loc.gov/2020028692

Milkweed Editions is committed to ecological stewardship. We strive to align
our book production practices with this principle and to reduce the impact of our
operations in the environment. We are a member of the Green Press Initiative, a
nonprofit coalition of publishers, manufacturers, and authors working to protect the
world's endangered forests and conserve natural resources. *We the Jury* was printed on
acid-free 100% postconsumer-waste paper by Friesens Corporation.

for
Stuart Friebert (1931–2020)
and Moikom Zeqo (1949–2020)

exceptional humanists

CONTENTS

My drama lies entirely . . . in my being conscious that each one of us believes himself to be a single person. But it's not true. . . .
—LUIGI PIRANDELLO

And whoever makes up the story makes up the world.
—ALI SMITH

WE THE JURY

THE NEWS

What nation has the most robust economy?

> *Death.*

And on what is that economy built?

> *The end of pain.*

What are Death's most notable exports?

> *Incompletion, oil,*
> *and the arts.*

What about imports?

> *Death is the largest consumer of voices—*
> *and, of course, bodies.*

What are Death's primary challenges?

> *It has none. Its economy*
> *is an inexorable machine.*

What then should our strategy be?

> *I'm afraid we have no choice*
>
> *but to expand our relationship*
> *with Death.*

And how do we do that?

> *We should ask:*
> *What are the needs of its citizens?*
>
> *Given our resources,*
> *What can we do for them?*

———

ON PROGRESS

I

My grandmother attended the last public hanging
in US history, which occurred
in Owensboro, Kentucky, in 1936.

She joined the crowd of 20,000
to see Rainey Bethea—Black and convicted
of rape, theft, and murder—hanged

by the first woman sheriff
in the history of the state. The draw
was not so much the execution, but that a woman

would be pulling the lever. In the end
Sheriff Thompson passed the job
to a former Louisville policeman

who showed up well dressed
and visibly drunk. To get to Owensboro,
my grandmother—Edna—

had ridden thirty-six miles
in one of her town's five cars.
A friend had convinced its owner,

a Mr. Hancock, to take them to the hanging,
where vendors would be selling
hot dogs, popcorn, and drinks.

2

The East Coast reporters raced home
to announce the barbarism
of those hilljacks and river people

who'd encircled, like a lamprey's mouth,
the gallows. Their multitude
had rushed forward to tear pieces

of Bethea's clothes, strips of his flesh.
A fight broke out over the hood,
the interior of which

was the last thing the dead man had seen—
echo of a mind
that suddenly no longer existed.

3

Eleven men are gathered
in the pictures on murderpedia.org
to erect the gallows. I must assume

the same craftsmanship and care
attend the raising of a gallows
as attend (e.g.) the framing of a house.

Look: on their lunch break
one of the men still chewing
bends to the joint between the steps

and the platform
and runs his eye along it.

4

In 1938 Edna eloped from her Baptist town
with a Catholic from across the river.
They left for Indianapolis

where the shame of their marriage
wouldn't follow. To me—as a child—
Grandma was gentle, quiet,

and strange. She slid through the house
in a pink nightgown. Her whole life
she was mentally ill. I don't mean

to imply she'd been affected
in some profound way by the prejudice
she and my grandfather received

or the violence she witnessed
that day in Owensboro. If asked, she'd say,
it was a fine afternoon, *the boy*

deserved what he got.

5

At least 1.6 million people have viewed online
the execution of Saddam Hussein.
I open the window and there he is

upright on the platform. The trapdoor drops
and the body pulls down against the life
that, since birth, has lifted its weight.

And then, in the world
across the screen, he's gone. Now
watch me pull back the scrubber bar—

his body lifted by the tip of my finger—
and let him drop again.

6

The condemned man
looking out on the crowd before him

must feel that every person there has become
inhuman. Why won't they rush forward
to save him? Impossible

this doesn't happen. Their attendance requires
they commit themselves
to the pure materiality

of his one body—as though a life
isn't still posted through it
and into the floor, holding him in place.

Then the trapdoor opens
and he never lands, like a cloud
of language—billowing till it's gone.

7

The crowd gathered for the killing
couldn't be more human; the condemned
is just no longer among them. My grandmother

died in 1998, having buried two husbands
and suffered a life of primitive
psychiatric treatments. I have no idea

how she comported herself
at Bethea's hanging. I can only see scenes
from the archives and imagine them

in motion inside her mind.

8

Child, look: we're building a house.
We're claiming space from the air,

celling it off, then moving through
as though we haven't just built
the floor we're standing on.

Clouds of language fill our rooms.
The neighbors think—
who really knows? Air branches

and unbranches inside us, this laden air
that fills our time. Then
the floor opens and we never land.

Built in the early twentieth century,
the barn stood across
from where the subdivision fence
pressed against the field.

We carried pliers and chainsaws,
crowbars and wrecking hammers.
We drove right up, bouncing
through the knee-high weeds.

First we tore off the stuck doors
then the box stalls. Our sorted
wood-scraps grew into piles.
When I pulled loose a long

board from the sheathing
the barn's century-old shadow
came apart. We dismantled it in strips
until the pale, compacted dirt

flooded with sun. The air
we'd opened there stayed sweet
and damp, even when a breeze
blew through. Next morning

Garrett went up the ladder
to pry down the rafters and purlins.
Then the barn was gone—
driven in shifts for two days

to Barnwood Recycling, who sold
the lumber to RiNo Development
for $4.75 a board foot. Clearly
the barn was not a metaphor.

It became the grayed interiors
of three restaurants, two of them
made from shipping containers.
More important,

it netted us $21,000,
my third of which helped my wife
and me pay for an IVF treatment—
which is also not a metaphor.

AFTER THE MISCARRIAGE

We sat in the car
—snow coming down—
just to get out of the house.

I lowered the window
sometimes to stop the snow
from sealing us in.

———————

The lights were still on
in those rooms where our daughter,
barely three, kept moving,
shifting her things.

———————

How many days—
weeks—did we leave her
in that lit-up silence?

———————

Back inside,
we let our footprints
melt on the floor.

She ran and hugged us
each entirely, as though

we'd come home after curfew
to this devoted,
oblivious parent.

OHIO, MY FRIENDS ARE DYING

I see their final days
in empty rooms

in that city
I left. See

their days as empty
rooms I left—

empty *because* I left.
Though, surely

their lives filled
with things

I can't see, filled,
as mine did elsewhere,

with time
that gathered to become

whatever their lives
meant to them.

Of course
more filled them

than heroin.
Days gathered

into a heavy lens
through which

I see my friends
blurred in those

abstract rooms
that suddenly emptied.

LITTLE DOMESTIC ELEGIES

I

When the backyard
light came on

I was surprised
to discover the air

filled with snow
so downy and silent

it never quite
reached the ground.

When the light went out,

all I could see
was solid dark

still full of that snow.

2

On our first cold day
in the new house

the clear world beyond us
became fogged

by the handprints
of whoever

had installed our windows.

3 .

Wind poured through

the framed-up house
they were building next door.

An emptiness
like photographic paper

waiting for some not-yet-
installed light

to turn on and imprint
the room

it has now become.

LOVE POEM

The purpose of the eye is to narrow
The world beyond the body
To a receptive point inside the body

At the center of the retina
The fovea centralis clusters half
The fibers of the optic nerve

Whatever light gets aimed to touch there
Comes from what the mind
Has focused on while the rest

Of the retina holds in periphery
Every other thing the mind can see
For this reason

When I found your glasses on the shelf
Where one of the kids could grab them
I picked them up

And put them out of reach

GENERATIONAL

Open the bays   and we fall together
as in archival footage

from last generation's war
we shift   inside our tumbling

the air hitting us
each   a little differently

there's comfort in this
collectivity   we'll land

together   more or less
our impacts   giving off

globes of light
becoming   one light

soundless   to the pilots
the bombardiers

wherever they've gone

CARILLON

Phones were ringing

in the pockets of the living
and the dead

the living stepped carefully among.
The whole still room

was lit with sound—like a switchboard—
and those who could answer

said hello. Then
it was just the dead, the living

trapped inside their clothes,
ringing and ringing them—

and this was
the best image we had

of what made us a nation.

—

TWO THOUSAND AND NINE

I

Those months we were no longer
making payments we felt
as if the rooms would stay ours
just because we moved through them.

That was our place in history:
our little house we lost which,
on the internet, remains a geometric cell
assigned a value as if from space.

Each night we carried the kids
up to their rooms, read them books,
sang them songs, then retired
to the deck to smoke and drink

and watch the windows come on
beyond the fence. We received
letter after letter; the ringing phone
pierced our life like a syringe.

When the sheriff's sale was imminent
we started pulling things out—
copper pipes, fixtures—whatever might
carry some value of that time

into the future. When we left
we put the kids in their seats and simply
backed out of the driveway,
just as we'd done all those years.

The rooms were stripped, the truck
was at my cousin's—and since
the moment had foreclosed on us
we'd find a new moment to slip into.

2

When the kids are in bed,
and you are in bed, and the shadows
of branches lick the wall above the table,

I open my laptop like a cellar door
onto that world stamped *image capture:
Mar 2009*—the neighborhood

when we lived there, the house
when we lived there. I scroll the streets
yard by yard, enter the shops on 75th

as if the past were a sealed room
that still exists. From one angle,
there's you on the porch

—face blurred out—
in a bright blouse I no longer
remember you owning.

STAGES ON A JOURNEY WESTWARD

I

All the mapmakers in history
have been wrong—

but to vastly differing degrees.

Mostly it hasn't mattered.

2

The old city thinning out, giving way
to strip malls and tar-seamed
parking lots—

and thinning inside me
already to images
glazed with feeling. Then

only fields around us
while back there the city
keeps moving, deep in its shadow.

3

Here in America
we are engines

drowning out what lies
beyond our interiors.

4

Alongside the interstate, a pumpjack
no taller than a quarter horse

just inside a pink
picket fence—

a pet!

5

When my daughter shit a cloud
into the motel pool

I leapt from the water
with her in my arms. A boy
pointed, yelling *Shit! Shit!*—

but half an hour later
no one else had gotten out.

6

This is America! the Irish
and Italians, the Greeks and Jews
and Poles were saying.

This is America! they cried.

Europe, then, was a dark room—
at its center a long
clawed-up table.

What is *this* America?

7

Four cows' soft faces
wedged through a metal gate—

flies like jewels crusting
their damp muzzles.

8

Then we pierced
our new city's
cloud of radio—

its stations
sleeping inside the dash
began to wake.

9

When everyone's asleep
I step into the yard. Around me

the ticking
of katydids. After all that

motion—the spinning tires,
the 1,200-mile sheath
of rushing air—

this dark bit of land
is a ticking engine.

MEETING THE BOARD

It was a beautiful antebellum house.
The servers were Black students of the university.
The silver was out and gibbous.
(All of this is true.)

One board member advised me in passing
that a teenage daughter shouldn't work—
she'd learn from her coworkers *criminal things*.
Instead, she should play soccer.

The chairman told us his dream
to gather the faculty in the conference center
for a day of unified prayer.

Our conversation turned, briefly, to the poor
trapped inside the hurricane—
which flashed its lightning
into different cities at different times.

Those people are never prepared,
explained a board member's coiffed wife.

The occasion was to mark a recent
departmental success that no one expected
the board to find interesting.

The room was a capsule of their power
they were obliged to inhabit
before departing for their sealed (and, I assume,
magnificent) box seats above the stadium.

For that hour, their approval engulfed us
like kudzu. They admired our work, they said—
and, understanding the balance
required of their position,

not to mention the impotence of literature,
if they read it, they would probably
admire this poem.

THE LENS

Let's admit   the past
was better than today   the clothes
were better   our lives
were better   we loved
more deeply   our voices
swelled with words that were larger

more clearly *us*   the cities
were cheaper   more bustling
the people kinder
we were smarter back then

before the kids   riskier more passionate
less sealed in ourselves   .
the government   was a light
that flooded our weapons
(which now have gone dark)

the poor knew their place
they worked   to climb out of it
there was an order   back

when the apples were crisper   the loaves
less cloying   the doctors
more honest   in that time

when the nation   was younger
when you   were a mystery
when the tax rates   were fairer
we could buy a soda for 15¢

there in that vault   our future
lay just beyond the door
open   and luminous

with this exact   same
abstraction and longing

MIDDLE AGE

1

When we've just taken off,
and the distance between us and earth

is still understandable—a few cars
sliding along a duct of road,

all the differentiated roofs slipping back
into a flat suburban panel—

that is when I most acutely feel
the plane could crash.

2

I was lifting—the surface

of my sleep below
was falling rapidly away. The expanse

between my body and whatever
always lies beneath it kept increasing,

and I could feel the possibility of plunging
through that vastness into nothing.

Then I was in the dark of our room

with you, love, stirring,
and I eased back into this headlong

forward hurtling
                    that's a kind
of stillness.

THE FUTURE

I

A bird in the airport
hopping among our feet—

dun puffed chest,
a sparrow I think—

collecting bits of popcorn
beside the luggage

while invisible speakers
fill the air with names

of cities irrelevant
to the air outside

from which this bird
has become mysteriously

separated. What should
be done for her?—

little feathered heart,
little Dickinson maybe—

who won't let any of us
touch her. The light

is mostly natural light;
the high ceilings'

support beams
make the environment

not unsuitable. If only
she could be coaxed

down the jetway
and onto the plane

to take to the sky
inside our human

endeavor, wouldn't that
be a kind of release?

2

After we boarded
and settled into our seats,

after the lights dimmed
and the movie began,

the plane shifted
course imperceptibly—

disconnected now
from the narrow bit of earth

we expected to receive us.
When we landed

we were together
in that daze of arrival—

carried reflexively
by the moving sidewalk,

the sky train—until
I was already well

inside the city I must
assume was arriving

suddenly into each of us.
All around me:

palm trees, saguaros,
floating puffs of cloud—

and it became clear
we were in, of all places,

Phoenix.

SONG FROM THE BACK OF THE HOUSE

Pistons firing in the pans,
the heavy light of the salamander,
and over by the walk-in
Nell returns each hour
to punch the air
growing inside her dough—

while the guests on the floor
keep insisting across their plates
they're middle class—.
If they're so middle class,
what are those of us
working back here?

                                    Oh.

————

Then I should say: I want nothing
more than the smallest chance
that history might notice us.
It could etch a little something
on the gearing

of its machinery. The story
of individual bodies is always
collapse. Soon we'll scatter
like leaves across the lawns
of the powerful—lawns we'll make
pristine by disappearing.

THE RAPTURE: A SERMON

We, the elect,
will be lifted

into the purity of our politics,
lifted like smoke

into the upside-down
buckets of bells.

We'll ring
against each other, and that

will become
the noise of the nation

hanging over the fields,
the past

like bits of nerve
glowing in the soil

of the boundless prairie.
Not the families

whispering on their blankets
beneath the fireworks,

nor the lovers—
who fail to see

the primary purpose
of language. We'll rise above

the left-behind,
who live their days

inside our words
emanating

from radios, screens—
then somehow

when night reaches over
they'll turn us off

and lie
silent in their beds.

We'll try to lift them
toward our righteousness

but they will fasten
to their lives,

their children watching
as our god

of wrath—god of history—
comes

to sweep them away.

—

When the dog finally died, dad dug a hole beside the fence and buried her in a boot box.

She's gone, but she had a good life, mom said. *It's OK to be sad.*

———

Next day, the boy came into the kitchen holding the box in front of him. *She's not gone. She's still in there*, he said. *Look.*

Mom lifted the lid. *Sweetie, when things die, we give them back to the earth.*

And then we forget them there?

Yes—and no, dad replied. He put the box in the hole and covered it over. Together, they walked back to the house.

———

In the morning, the box was on the kitchen counter. *I couldn't sleep*, the boy said. *She was all alone out there.*

Maybe that's how she wants it to be, dad replied.

No. She doesn't want anything, the boy said. *She's dead. But her box was full of air inside the earth. That wasn't right.*

They filled the box with dirt and placed it inside the hole.

What does it mean to die? the boy asked.

Dad thought of his own father, who'd died a year before the boy was born. A long suffering—until at last his body had filled with snow.

No one knows what death is, dad said. _I wish I had a better answer for you._

———

Four days passed before the box, heavy with dirt and rot, arrived again inside the house. _Why is this here?_ dad asked.

No one knows what death is, the boy said. _I wanted to find out._

Jesus, dad said and went out to the garage.

Mom said gently, _No. When things die, they're gone. So we return them to the earth._

———

The dog was gone—that was clear.

But the dog was also right there, just below the surface, packed in darkness. The boy could bring her back inside whenever he wanted—

no matter what his parents said.

NOTES: HISTORY

1

This flower

detached from the pressurized
system of the shrub

stands frozen in time—

but a bit of tap water
will draw up through the stem

and compel the petals
to continue opening.

2

I'm saying this
from inside your mind,

having carried
myself into you

through the dust
of the Roman alphabet.

3

The mice living in the walls

belong entirely
to the house.

4

When a hollow top is spun,
the air inside it

also spins.

5

That obscure Wyeth print

my father bought
as a student—

I found the actual painting
in the Denver Art Museum,

blocks from where I've moved
long past my father's death.

Not sure what else to do,
I took its picture with my phone.

6

Leaves fallen to the surface
of a lake

will float for some time
before sinking.

7

To the people rounded up
and stood against a wall

it couldn't have mattered less
that the other side

was just over there.

8

I was surprised to see steam
coming off the floodlights

lifting the field from the dark.

I'd thought of them
as generating light, not heat.

9

The fighter jet flying overhead
holds three stories at once:

that of the war,
that of the plane,
and that of the pilot.

10

A Fourth of July parade
feels like a cohesive thing

that has, for the moment,
rendered the street inviolable—

but it's easy just to run
through a gap in the procession.

11

According to the documentary,

after the war was over, the bomb craters
that had filled with rainwater

became ponds
exploding with lilies—

and then a golf course was designed
around these perfect
natural obstacles.

12

There were, at first, just a few drops of rain,

and we could discern
their sounds as they landed.

Then, there was only rain.

RAIN STUDY

1

All night, the channeling of water
in the gutters

keeps tracing
the outline of the house.

2

My son's face pressed
to one side of the glass,
the storm to the other.
He's too young

to understand
why the trees
swing around in nightmare
mechanical motion—

but the rain
filling the air before him
must have something
to do with it. Each

flash of lightning
brings the present

more sharply
into the present. He turns back

to our space inside it.

3

It was raining in the capital
and the nation's new delight—

the war—was on.

A thick fuzz of rain
stood on its pintips

in every street. The awnings
hung their empty rooms

like diving bells
inside that falling.

4

Again, my daughter is talking

in her sleep—her language
just water
cycling through a fountain.

And my son, who can't yet speak—
endless rain.

5

Then my wife and I
were alone in the house

for the first time in months—
a shocking quiet

dampened further by the gray
of rain. When the wind gusted,

a drop sometimes
landed in a square

of the bedroom's
window screen. Later

the scattered
placement of water there

offered a record
of the afternoon.

6

On the undersurface
of a raindrop
as it falls:

a fisheyed reflection
of the ground
rising at tremendous speed

and that's it—

MIDDLE AGE

I

This body, which equals a life—
no more, no less—
and, thus, is incomplete,
even asleep, even watching TV,

soon will rise
to pee, to find itself
in the mirror examining
what this body appears to be.

And I was wrong thinking
time gathers inside me.
I was wrong inside my body
moving through time.

So that now I imagine
a dot matrix print head
growing a picture, each pass
revealing one more line

of body until
the image is whole—
and then some other body
must come and dispose of it.

2

At my one-week
follow-up appointment

I listened to the person
who had opened

for the first time ever
my abdominal cavity—

grown from nothing
like the hollow of a pepper.

I watched her fingers
hold a plastic pen

that marked on a pad
her swoops of thought.

The light around us
had poured into my body,

annihilating its darkness
where no one lives.

TWO SISTERS

In the photo, the woman on the left is dying,
the woman on the right is well.

They look nearly the same—
same features and hair, same t-shirts—

and the backlit space between them
seems to float, like Rubin's vase.

In six months one sister will appear unchanged;
and one will be waxy, hair nearly gone.

But here the world feels large—
you can see it—and after the shutter snaps,

that shape their bodies have made
together in the air   will disappear

as they cross the lawn toward
the rest of us gathered on the porch.

MIND-BODY PROBLEM

When I touch your skin and goosebumps lift,
it's your mind that surfaces there.
When your iris tightens mechanically
around your pupil, that aperture
becomes for me the blacked-out
cockpit of your mind.
                          It's your mind
that touches your tongue to mine,
your mind that, when you're driving,
lowers your hand to my thigh
almost mindlessly.
                          Your mind
like a pilot light inside your sleep,
your mind that beats your heart—
slower, then faster—infusion pump
in the chest, flooding your mind.

But your heart is not your mind.
The curve of your hip; the soft
skin of your wrist is not your mind.
The tumor growing in your brain
is just your brain, I say.
                          The shape
of your face; the sound of your voice,
which I love so much, is not your mind.
Your mind spills through—fire

I can't stop watching from the far
side of this darkening valley.

When his friend's last notes and letters
arrived in a heavy envelope, he found
more than a hundred pages bound
simply with a rubber band. For three hours
he dragged his mind through the strands
of her tight cursive. He was surprised
that he recognized almost none
of the thoughts and events related there.

He'd assumed he would gain a clearer
vision of her lost interior
but in the end so little was revealed
he decided the reading had barely
counted, even, as reading. It was more
like combing her hair.

FROM THE AFTERLIFE OF THE RICH

I

We were rich. In the valley below,
the highway formed a pavé river

and down in the orchestra pit
the musicians were clothed in our
sustaining contributions.

Our portfolios swelled and contracted
inside digital ribcages
and that silent breathing

was the breathing of a spirit that's
beyond you. When we left,
our houses filled with security—

mute and clear, like still water.
When we returned, that presence
withdrew into our secret codes.

All summer long, a mist
rose off our lawns—I'm sure
you'd say like steam resurfacing

from a buried 19th century.
(It was recycled water,
on a timer, for the grass.)

2

We were *the rich*. We glimpsed the poor
smoking dumbly on their stoops,

lugging gas cans to their drained vehicles.
We filled their televisions

as though we were
fictional characters. We recalled
their revolutionary songs, we could see

them covet our luxury hybrids.
They looked up to us, you know,

with the blankness of a field
of tiny flowers. When they agitated,
it was like a breeze

out of nowhere passed across
their surface. That trembling was lovely

when observed from a distance.
In a minute it would stop.

3

But our lives, too, were visited
by elemental tragedies: deaths of parents,

illnesses of children, fires
that absolutely failed to light. Poet,

with your miniscule economy
simply no one understands,

I know what you'll say: your art
was there for us, and yes, *it was.*

More important, in those moments
of terror and empty, useless grief

our primary need
was sympathy—real sympathy—

which we, like all the living,
deserved.

—

ON HISTORY

I

In December 1961, George Trabing
shot Winifred Jean Whittaker

and left her body beside the Trinity River
in one of the long twin shadows
of the I-10 overpass.

In August 1988, George Trabing
took me out on Trinity Bay
in his twenty-five-foot sloop
and taught me how to sail.

Past the bridge he cut the engine
and I felt us lock suddenly into the wind
dragging overhead—invisible,
unrelenting machine.

2

Trabing was in a "narcotics-fueled frenzy"
when he murdered Whittaker

while searching for more drugs
"on the Negro side of town"; when he

attempted to assault a fourteen-year-old girl,
then returned her home;

when he burglarized a house in wealthy
River Oaks for $7. In the subsequent trial,

which lasted three months,
the prosecutor sought the death penalty

but did not succeed.

3

The Trinity River enters Trinity Bay
by way of the Anahuac Channel,

which was cut through the marsh-pocked delta
by the Army Corps of Engineers

and on the map looks like a straw
thrust into the bay's broad bladder.

Those afternoons George took me sailing,
I don't believe we ever went over

to that other side of the bay.

4

He drank cans of beer from a plastic cooler;
I drank 7-Up. He taught me to tie knots
and watch the mainsail for luffing.
Those afternoons

were a favor to my father, who still had to work
while I was visiting from Ohio.

George—who'd become a professor
after fifteen years in prison—
had his summers off.

5

Trabing was finally arrested
in the lobby of the Auditorium Hotel,
which, I'm shocked to discover,

became the Lancaster—and where,
on September 10, 2001, I had drinks
after seeing Salman Rushdie read.

The event was picketed
by fundamentalists; police barricades
maintained a channel through the crowd.

I don't remember what Rushdie read
or anything he said. I remember
passing through that compacted organ of anger

and into the vast theater,
red and plush and radiant with money.
The protesters remained outside,

and Rushdie was the only person
facing their direction as he spoke—
and, of course,

it was September 10, 2001.

6

The family of Winifred Jean Whittaker
must despise George Trabing—
who is surely both abstract

and the very most powerful expression
of *real*. They would be right to say
it was a racist travesty of justice

he became a professor
and remained for the rest of his life
in Houston—their town—walking free

with his title and the prestige it carried.
They must find it horrific
he could spend twenty years running

a master's program for prisoners,
that he had the means and time
to own a boat and teach a boy to sail.

7

My god, why did my father
let George Trabing take me out
alone on his boat?

To show friendship, to offer trust?
As a teenager, my father

had wanted to be a priest,
though by 1988 he'd long become
an unshakeable atheist. I know George

was his good friend and no doubt
dad thought I would enjoy sailing.

Beyond that, it was a religious decision—
an atavism, a proof of faith—
I'm pretty sure.

8

Dare I say?—

Of the men I spent time with as a child,
George was among the very kindest
and most generous—and he offered me
a respectfulness I didn't, at twelve, deserve.

I sometimes flip through the *Royce's
Sailing Illustrated* he gave me,
and I recall his insistence
that a sloop rolled by the wind

would quickly right itself. Surely
he said that only to allay my fear

when the boat heeled hard and I yelped,
thinking we were going over.
He is to me both an abstraction

and a very powerful expression
of *real*. Which is why I'm still here

in the library so late in the afternoon,
retrieving articles from 1961–2
on "George Trabing."

WE THE JURY

having heard the evidence against us

having taken into account the strength of every possible position

having gone home to our partners our children

and having never mentioned the full details of our thoughts

having come to comprehend the wrongs of which we stand accused

having pledged to consider our omissions and our acts

we know that *we* will determine the facts

and those facts will become the surface

upon which this world rests   we will assess

the veracity of our witnessing against us   we understand

our innocence could well require we find ourselves guilty

and when at last the verdict arrives

we will come down upon us with the weight of our entire existence

even then   not one of us

will truly understand what we have done

The war stopped precisely
where it was. Soldiers
mortared foundations
inside their fighting positions—
then they erected walls,
then windows and roofs. At night

they gazed from their bedrooms
down into the valley
with its dim town
they'd failed to enter. Trenches
swelled with rainwater;
soon punts and tour boats
slipped over the dugouts.

So many of the structures
we lived among—that shaped
our days—belonged to the war.
Tanks packed with silence
rested in the square. Bombers
hovered—frozen—
above their targets,

and the children wondered
at what was up there.
They began climbing the ladders
of bombs hanging from the sky—
and when the most daring of them

reached the bays to clamber
finally into the cockpits, the war
snapped back into motion.

THE REENACTMENT

When the dog ran out onto the field

between the opposing lines
of uniformed men
a few squat cannons
muskets cantilevered into the air

a boy chased it
from among the colony of lawn chairs
t-shirts and gym shoes

that in that context represented
a more fully comprehending vantage

and for a moment the battle continued
muskets popping men shouting
period curses and commands

while the boy and his dog
filled the smoke-hazed pitch with their chase
the leash trailing through grass
the boy calling *Buster Buster*

until the guns slowed then stopped
and a few soldiers broke from their sides
to chase the dog too

and then one of them trapped the leash
beneath his boot so the animal
jerked to a halt

and the dog and child were led
triumphantly from the battlefield

toward the bright colors of the future
where we all now
were standing to receive them

After the economic summit,
he spent three more evenings
in the cafes across from the cathedral
drinking wine and coffee
and marveling at the age of things.

He touched the abbey's leaded glass,
far older than the Constitution,
he paused beneath the storm
painted high inside the cupola. Even
his hotel was older than America.

He had no idea the city
had been firebombed in the war,
walls crumbled, roofs burned,
that rain for months had filled
the very room he slept in.

The Roman ruins had been reduced
almost to nothing and later
were restored. *You Americans*,
the waiter had said, *always looking up
at the old buildings*. That night

he stood on a medieval bridge
(built in 1951, from pictures
in the archives) and could feel it
lift him above the modern world,
a fog of voices in the plaza.

THE NARCISSIST

Our boats on the black water, and the lighthouse
swinging its gaze around, its beam
reaching and withdrawing, reaching
and withdrawing. It seemed
the whole sea rose up
to that towering eye.
                  It seemed as though
it had the power to draw
us from our shadows,
to lure us toward the rocks the waves
were breaking hard against. What would we do
if we got there?
                  But we were farther
away than we'd supposed—and when that blaze
of light slid briefly across us
it only served to show us to each other.

AT TODAY'S AUSCHWITZ,

someone must be the director. Someone
must maintain the structures
against the appetites of nature,

must tuckpoint the blockhouses,
the officers' quarters, must replace
the glass and keep the windows clean.

Must walk the halls,
having reconstructed the halls, must
enter the showers and visit the ovens,

must inspect the barbed wire
for rust and replace it. Must rebuild
the guard towers, remake the signs

with their stenciled letters,
retrace the shallow
etchings along the bunks. Someone

who lives in Katowice,
or Wadowice, a team of someones
must change the lightbulbs,

must unclog the toilets
when crowds pour through the gates.
Must safeguard the shoes,

the tangles of eyeglasses, must
raise the flag above the courtyard.
Our cities keep tumbling forward,

trees push into the air without us,
birds pierce the agar of silence
inside which a man patrols

a field of chimneys—taking notes
for the work ahead—then goes home
to his quiet, lit-up street.

THE HUMANIST

When he rose before the jury of his peers
he knew he had arrived at the endgame
of his belief, mirror against mirror,

and when they read to him his crimes—
his betrayal of the time's
consensus—he saw he would be folded into the body

of the human story. He would be
judged and found guilty
of elevating men to this very position of judgment.

The loneliest person on earth
is a humanist condemned. When the pyre
was lit, it bloated the square

with light—the light his body fed.
Later the guards cleaned up in darkness.
We have no record of what they said.

NOTES

Epigraphs: Pirandello's *Six Characters in Search of an Author*, trans. Frederick May; Ali Smith's *Autumn*.

"The American Middle Class" is indebted to Conor O'Callaghan's "Wild Strawberries," which ends with the insistence "They're not metaphors. / They are not metaphors."

"Ohio, My Friends Are Dying" is for K. and B.

"Carillon": June 12, 2016.

"Two Sisters": Danish psychologist Edgar Rubin's well known black-and-white optical illusion. For A. and J.

"At Today's Auschwitz" is indebted to Wisława Szymborska's "The End and the Beginning" (trans. Stanisław Barańczak and Clare Cavanagh), which repeats the line "Someone's got to . . ." According to a 2018 study conducted by The Conference on Jewish Material Claims Against Germany, 41% of Americans and 66% of American millennials can't identify what Auschwitz was. A quick Google search tells me that Piotr Cywiński does the work of directing the Auschwitz-Birkenau State Museum and that Jolanta Banaś-Maciaszczyk directs the Preservation Department; this poem is for them.

ACKNOWLEDGMENTS

Thanks to the editors of the following publications, where these poems first appeared, sometimes in earlier versions and/or with different titles: *Academy of American Poets Poem-a-Day*: "Carillon" and "Mind-Body Problem"; *The Adroit Journal*: "Rain Study"; *American Poetry Review*: "Little Domestic Elegies" and "Love Poem"; *Boulevard*: "From the Afterlife of the Rich" and "The Lens"; *Conduit*: "An American Abroad" and "We the Jury"; *Crazyhorse*: "Meeting the Board"; *Field*: "After the Miscarriage" and "Two Sisters"; *Horsethief*: "At Today's Auschwitz" and "Middle Age [This body]"; *The Literary Review*: "The News," "The Rapture: A Sermon," and "Song from the Back of the House"; *The Los Angeles Review*: "The American Middle Class," "Invention of the Afterlife," and "The Narcissist"; *Memorious*: "Middle Age [When we've just taken off]"; *New England Review*: "On Progress"; *Plume*: "Stages on a Journey Westward" and "Two Thousand and Nine"; *Poetry Northwest*: "Notes: History"; *The Southern Review*: "Parable of Childhood"; *Subtropics*: "On History"; *Tupelo Quarterly*: "The Future" and "The Reenactment"; *32 Poems*: "Generational" and "The Humanist"; *Waxwing*: "Armistice" and "Ohio, My Friends Are Dying."

"On Progress" was listed as "notable" in the *Pushcart Prize: Best of the Small Presses 2018* anthology. "From the Afterlife of the Rich," "Generational," and "The Humanist" were reprinted on *Poetry Daily*. "We the Jury" was reprinted on *Verse Daily*. "Meeting the Board" and "Mind-Body Problem" were reprinted in *Poetry International*. "The

Humanist," "After the Miscarriage," "Ohio, My Friends Are Dying," and "Carillon" were reprinted in the poetry section of the *Colorado Encyclopedia*. "Mind-Body Problem" was reprinted on the website of the Norwegian Writers' Climate Campaign.

My profound thanks to Kevin Prufer for being these poems' first reader, and to Joy Katz, Randall Mann, and Michael Bazzett, who read this book in manuscript and offered invaluable edits, comments, and advice. Deep and continuing gratitude to Daniel Slager, as well as to the rest of the brilliant people at Milkweed Editions. I'm grateful to my excellent colleagues Brian Barker, Nicky Beer, and Joanna Luloff, and to the University of Colorado Denver for its unflagging support. Thanks to those who listened, advised, suggested books to read, offered encouragement, and/or generally were fellow travelers—particularly (but not exclusively) Hadara Bar-Nadav, Justin Boening, Jericho Brown, Victoria Chang, Martha Collins, David J. Daniels, Murray Farish, Graham Foust, John Gallaher, Sean Hill, Henry Israeli, Ben Johnson, Ilya Kaminsky, Alex Lemon, Ada Limón, Rebecca Lindenberg, Erika Meitner, Sinéad Morrissey, Kathryn Nuernberger, Paul Perry, D. A. Powell, Chris Santiago, Martha Serpas, Stephen Sexton, Craig Morgan Teicher, and Devon Walker-Figueroa. Special thanks to the Zeqo-Miraj family. In memoriam, Michelle Boisseau and Ciaran Carson, each of whom commanded an essential "small back room." My love and deepest gratitude to Jeanne, Harper, and Sean: my world.

WAYNE MILLER is the author of *Post-* (2016), winner of the Rilke Prize and the Colorado Book Award; *The City, Our City* (2011), shortlisted for the Rilke Prize and the William Carlos Williams Award; *The Book of Props* (2009), named a best poetry book of the year by *Coldfront Magazine* and the *Kansas City Star*; and *Only the Senses' Sleep* (2006), winner of the William Rockhill Nelson Award. He has received the George Bogin Memorial Award, the Lucille Medwick Memorial Award, the Lyric Poetry Award, a Ruth Lilly Fellowship, the Bess Hokin Prize, and a Fulbright Distinguished Scholarship to the Seamus Heaney Centre at Queen's University Belfast. He is co-translator of two books by the Albanian writer Moikom Zeqo—most recently *Zodiac* (2015), which was shortlisted for the PEN Center USA Award in Translation—and co-editor of three books: *Literary Publishing in the Twenty-First Century* (2016), *Tamura Ryuichi: On the Life & Work of a 20th Century Master* (2011), and *New European Poets* (2008). He teaches at the University of Colorado Denver, co-directs the Unsung Masters Series, and serves as editor/managing editor of *Copper Nickel*.

milkweed
editions

Founded as a nonprofit organization in 1980,
Milkweed Editions is an independent publisher.
Our mission is to identify, nurture and publish
transformative literature, and build an engaged
community around it.

Milkweed Editions is based in Bde Ota (Minneapolis)
within Mní Sota Makoče, the traditional homeland
of the Dakhóta people. Residing here since time
immemorial, Dakhóta people still call Mní Sota Makoče
home, with four federally recognized Dakhóta nations
and many more Dakhóta people residing in what is now
the state of Minnesota. Due to continued legacies of
colonization, genocide, and forced removal, generations
of Dakhóta people remain disenfranchised from their
traditional homeland. Presently, Mní Sota Makoče has
become a refuge and home for many Indigenous nations
and peoples, including seven federally recognized Ojibwe
nations. We humbly encourage readers to reflect upon the
historical legacies held in the lands they occupy.

milkweed.org

Interior design and tyepesetting
by Mary Austin Speaker
Typeset in Adobe Caslon
Adobe Caslon Pro was created by Carol Twombly
for Adobe Systems in 1990. Her design was inspired by
the family of typefaces cut by the celebrated engraver
William Caslon I, whose family foundry served
England with clean, elegant type from the early
Enlightenment through the turn of the
twentieth century.